Southwood House during World War One

HEART OF SOUTHWOOD

A History and Appreciation
of Price's Avenue and Southwood Neighbourhood,
Ramsgate

2007

Every effort has been made to ensure that the content of this work is correct.   However, no guarantee is given as to the accuracy of any part of it. Fresh information appears from time to time, and I therefore propose to keep the work open to revision.

Steve Moore - January 2007

Heart Of Southwood

First Published by
Michaels Bookshop
Ramsgate
2007
© Steve Moore

ISBN: 1-905477-88-0
ISBN 13: 978-1905477-88-3

Introduction

The precise extent of the once wooded area from which Southwood in the town of Ramsgate takes its name is uncertain. Today, Southwood has much clearer definition in the local inhabitant's mental map as a predominantly residential area and as the home ground of Ramsgate football. It equates with the area of the former Southwood Farm and of Southwood House. Southwood's large, Victorian water tower is also one of Ramsgate's distinctive and prominent landmarks.

The Southwood neighbourhood occupies an area of about half a square kilometre, and consists predominantly of late nineteenth and early twentieth century houses. It sits on elevated ground one kilometre to the west of Ramsgate town centre and behind the more prestigious houses, cliff-top promenades and greens of the West Cliff area.

Southwood is adjoined to its north by Saint Lawrence, which marks the site of the earliest local settlement in Ramsgate. (Ramsgate itself developed first as a fishing hamlet at a natural dip in the chalk cliffs, and grew later principally as a resort). Once a tiny hamlet, which preceded but later developed around the parish church, Saint Lawrence, like Southwood, has since been assimilated into Ramsgate as the town developed. Both Southwood and Saint Lawrence retain some sense of identity, the latter reinforced by the dominant presence of its church.

Southwood actually evolved first as a separate hamlet in otherwise open farmland, and then became "built up" with housing around the turn of the century. The area cannot therefore be regarded as of such historic importance and general interest as, for example, Ramsgate Harbour or the concentrations of Regency housing around the town centre which more directly reflect the historic origins and development of the town. These aspects have been admirably recorded in a number of works (including, notably, "The book of Ramsgate" by Charles Busson)

I have very fond memories of Southwood and, as a small boy, frequently visited my grandparents' house there in Price's Avenue. These visits were often accompanied by visits to the beach and town or by leisurely days in the sunny back garden. Even at that early age, the attractive and characteristic qualities of the house and those in its immediate neighbourhood intrigued me and left a considerable impression. Largely unchanged today, the area retains a distinct sense of place, with an almost uncanny ability to evoke these pleasant recollections. More objectively, few would disagree that the neighbourhood offers a pleasant residential environment of some character.

This study has developed from my great interest in and affection for Southwood and, in particular, the houses in Price's Avenue. It aims to piece together a bit about the history and development of the roads, buildings and architecture which provide the area with its pleasant character. The study begins with the early nineteenth century, when most of Southwood was arable farmland.

I hope that the work will be of some local interest especially to those living in or having associations with Southwood and especially Price's Avenue neighbourhood, where I now live, and which, for me, will always be the "Heart" of Southwood.

General view of Southwood from Saint Laurence Church tower - 2006

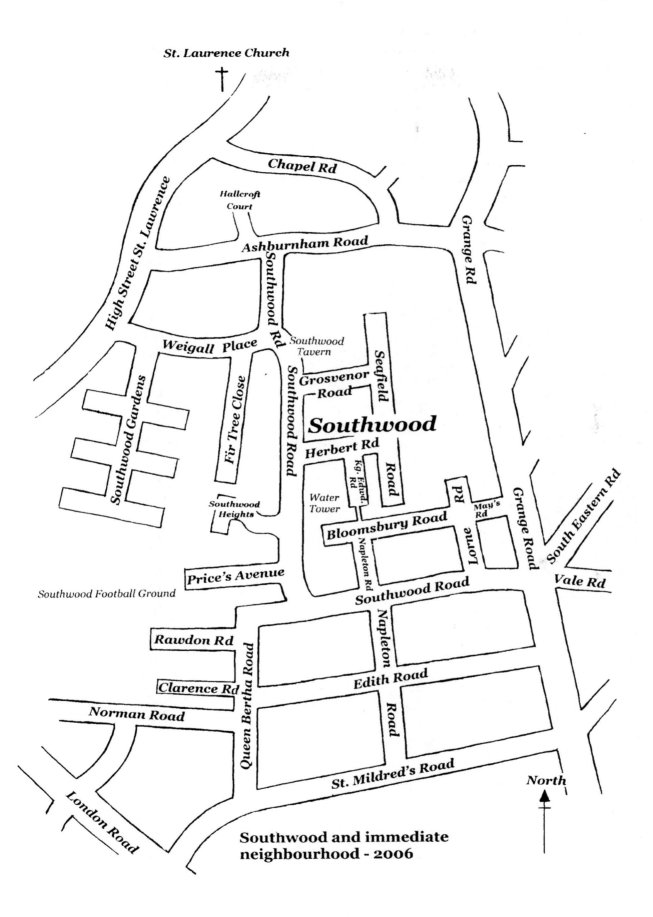

St. Laurence Church

Chapel Rd

Hallcroft Court

Ashburnham Road

High Street St. Lawrence

Southwood Rd

Weigall Place

Southwood Tavern

Seafield

Grosvenor Road

Southwood

Southwood Gardens

Fir Tree Close

Southwood Road

Herbert Rd

Road

Southwood Heights

Water Tower

Kg. Edmd. Rd

Bloomsbury Road

Napleton Rd

Lorne

Pd

May's Rd

Grange Road

South Eastern Rd

Price's Avenue

Southwood Football Ground

Southwood Road

Vale Rd

Rawdon Rd

Queen Bertha Road

Napleton

Clarence Rd

Edith Road

Norman Road

Road

St. Mildred's Road

North

London Road

Grange Rd

Southwood and immediate neighbourhood - 2006

CHAPTER 1 - Southwood Farm

Price's Avenue is perhaps best locally known as the access road to the Ramsgate Football Ground, and for its somewhat quaint, attractive little dwelling, "Swiss Cottage". The Avenue consists of a short cul-de-sac situated about halfway along Southwood Road, which threads through the Southwood neighbourhood.

The land now occupied by Price's Avenue and much of built-up Southwood, was previously agricultural land, attached to Southwood Farm. Until 1805 the Farm was owned by George Osborne Sayer. The map below shows how Southwood looked at around this time. (The pecked square relates to area of the map on the preceding page)

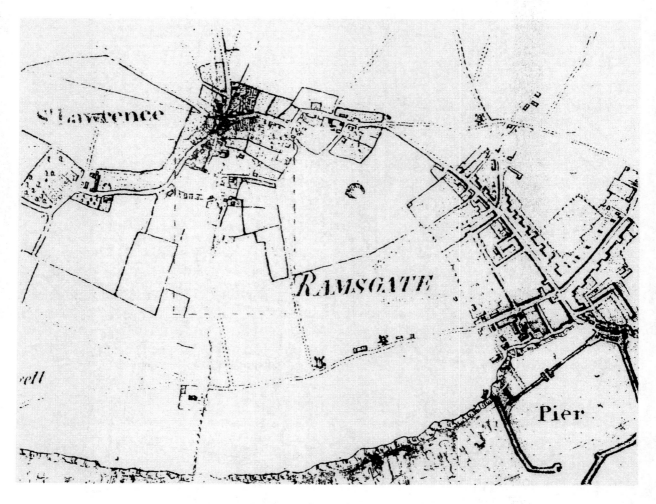

Map circa 1800 (Source ref 1)

After George Sayer died, Southwood Farm was inherited by his brother Richard. It later passed to Sarah Sayer (Richard Sayer's wife). The Farm buildings were situated behind the present Southwood Tavern, and the extent of the Farm is shown on the Plan dated Mid 19th Century. It is uncertain whether the Farm was actually known as South Wood Farm (as opposed to Southwood Farm) or whether this was simply an error on the auction plan!

View across Southwood Farm showing Southwood House - 1812
(Source ref 2)

The southern and western boundaries of the site which became Price's Avenue (then a small parcel in arable use) formed the outer extent of Southwood Farm. The land to the north of that parcel also once formed part of the Farm. However, in around 1835 a reservoir was built on it following formation of the Ramsgate Waterworks Company, (see Chapter 8). North of this stood Southwood House. (see Chapter 2)

To its south, the Price's Avenue land was abutted by a slightly larger arable enclosure. In about 1843 this was owned by Joseph Templeman; then owner and occupier of Southwood House. Around 1847 however, this land evidently belonged to J. A. Warre, and was probably attached to the now converted farm buildings called "The Homestead" (off London Road). In the middle of the century, the plot was developed with a large house (see Chapter 3). A path along its eastern boundary, which separated it from Southwood Farm, later became Queen Bertha Road.

The land to the west of the Price's Avenue site, then known as "Chilton Field", extended down to the present site of Nethercourt roundabout and was in the ownership of Benjamin Bushel and occupation of Thomas Mayhew. Nearby Nethercourt Farm was then in similar ownership and tenancy. Mr Mayhew (1798-1897) managed the Nethercourt Farm business on behalf of his uncle. Part of the land later became Southwood Football Ground, (See Chapter 7)

Southwood Farm Sold

Sarah Sayer died in around May 1847, having willed that (at least part of) the farm be shared equally between her son George Sayer and another party upon trust that their part of the land be sold at auction as considered expedient by their trustees. The Farm was auctioned that same year at the Albion Hotel, Ramsgate.

The farmland was divided into seven separate lots presumably to maximise its sale value as building land. The parcel of land which was to become Price's Avenue was sold as a separate lot (Lot 3). Just prior to sale, "Lot 3" was in the occupation of Mr. Bailey (a yearly tenant). It was already separately enclosed; then being surrounded on three sides by land in different ownerships, and bounded to its east by the track which later became Southwood Road.

Lot 3 was purchased for a price of £400. The details of sale note that it was believed to be brick earth, and that one acre of it had already been sold for £300. Available records indicate that a purchaser named "Witherden" bought Lots 1 - 3. After its sale, Lot 3 was worked as a brick field

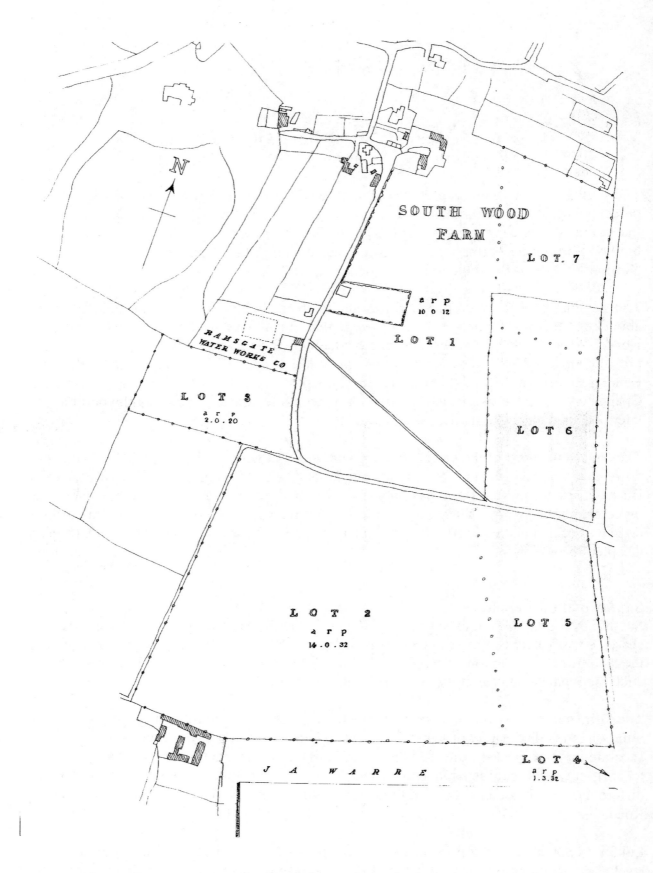

Mid 19th Century Plan showing Auction Lots Of Land At South Wood Farm.
Source ref 3

The next three Chapters look at some of the more distinguished and notable houses that pre-date much of built-up Southwood.

CHAPTER 2 - Southwood House

The area now occupied by Southwood Gardens previously formed the site and gardens of Southwood House. This house was indisputably the most famous and largest residence in Southwood.

Southwood House was built by a Captain Cotton who acquired the site, then occupied by two small cottages, and much of the land around it, in 1720. The house was sold to a Captain Burns who added the left wing and promptly sold it on to a Peter Burgess (one of the first elected commissioners for Ramsgate). Improvements were made with successive owners and the house became very sizeable.

An advertisement of 1795 described Southwood House as being "Most desirable in situation, commanding uninterrupted views of the Downs and coasts of France, and the whole encircled with lofty brick walling and fit for the reception of a genteel family".

Southwood House 1812
(source ref 2)

It was at Southwood House that the Earl and Countess of Dunmore found a seaside residence. Their unhappy daughter, separated from the husband (the Duke of Sussex) to whom she believed herself legally married, joined them in Thanet at a house (since demolished) on the Ramsgate cliffs. The "Baroness D'Ameland", as she was called, was given her royal title by the sympathetic inhabitants of Ramsgate, though the King steadfastly refused to acknowledge her as the Duchess Of Sussex. The Countess of Dunmore died at Southwood House, and her tomb, together with that of her daughter and her two children is in St Lawrence Churchyard.

The tithe map of 1843 shows the house was then owned and occupied by Joseph Templeman. The House was subsequently purchased by the Dowager Countess of Ashburnham, daughter of the Duke of Northumberland, who died in 1865. Ashburnham Road in Southwood is named after her.

In August 1880 Southwood House was bought by Henry and Rose Weigall, and it was to remain the home of the Weigalls for the next forty years. The house was later demolished and redeveloped with the housing at Southwood Gardens (Chapter 11).

Rose Weigall's life is recorded through the recollections of friends and correspondence in "Lady Rose Weigall" by her daughter, Rachel Weigall (published 1923). As a notable inhabitant of Southwood, any study of its history would be incomplete without reference to her busy, influential and philanthropic life.

Lady Rose Weigall (from a portrait by her husband Henry Weigall 1867 - source ref 4)

Rose Sophia Mary Weigall (nee Fane) was the youngest daughter of John, Lord Burghersh, afterwards Earl Of Westmorland. Her mother, Priscilla, was related to the Duke Of Wellington who evidently had great affection for Rose and her parents. Lord Burghersh served with distinction in the Napoleonic Wars, after which he was appointed Minister at Florence. In 1830, opposed to political reforms, he resigned and returned to England. It was here at Hyde Park Terrace 1834 that Rose was born. Five years later Lord Berghersh was appointed Minister at Belgium where Rose received her education and developed a love of history. When Rose was seventeen her father was appointed to the Embassy of Vienna where at coming out age she enjoyed "society" life but remained committed to intellectual improvement, studying Italian, drawing and enjoying classic literature. She also assisted her father, acting as an extra secretary in his conferences and negotiations in respect of the Crimean War.

Lord Berghersh later retired from diplomacy to settle again at the village of Apethorpe in England. It was here that Rose developed an involvement in social work. One year after the death of Lord Westmorland, the family moved back to London and back into the intellectual and political circles of society life. She met Henry Weigall, then at the height of his career as a portrait painter, at a ball given by the Duchess Of Cleveland. She married Henry Weigall on 15th August 1866 at Westminster Abbey. This was evidently a remarkable service with celestial music rendered by a choir of harps.

Henry and Rose Weigall lived at Bryanstone Square until the death of Lady Westmorland broke the chief tie with London. They then sought a country home. Henry Weigall had already built a house for summer use at Westgate (the first on the sea front) and the picturesque coast and bracing air of Thanet had already made their appeal. When the roomy Southwood House with its large garden came on the market Henry Weigall bought it. Rachel Weigall recalls that Southwood was a very full and noisy household. Her father's studio was detached from the house so that he could work undisturbed.

While the immediate claims of home remained her priority, Rose Weigall devoted astonishing levels of personal commitment to social work, initiating and carrying on improvements of all kinds. The local foundation of this work was the Minster Workhouse, which Rose regularly visited, taking books, flowers and papers to cheer the inmates.

From 1881 an annual treat was instituted at Southwood. The children and old people of the workhouse would be brought to the house in a procession of horse charabancs "with much cheering and waving of flags". The afternoon was spent in games, swings and donkey rides in the cricket field at the end of the garden, followed by tea on the lawn. Afterwards there was Punch and Judy, and each child was given a present before departure.

When grown up, Rose's children established a local "Southwood" cricket team. Matches held at the house were open to neighbours to spectate and accompanied by the informal hospitality of tea on the lawn

Southwood House

Lady Rose managed a local training home "Dover House", enabling girls to train for domestic service as an alternative to the workhouse. Henry Weigall provided a country holiday facility at Southwood for poor children, including lads trained and sent out as pantry and house boys. Such holiday lodgings were expensive and farm buildings were not easily available. However, a large loft over the Southwood stables was adapted for such use, and, later a dedicated camp facility accommodating sixty bed spaces, kitchen and dining tables was built on half an acre of waste ground adjoining a large field attached to the house.

Lady Rose also maintained her foreign connections and an interest in foreign politics. During the War she involved herself, through the Red Cross and the censor, in tracing missing individuals of all ranks on behalf of anxious families, and lobbying to improve conditions for prisoners of war. Even the German bombardment did not deter her from remaining at Southwood and continuing her work. However, in 1917 the house was rendered uninhabitable by damage from an aerial torpedo from a Zeppelin, and the family moved away until the following year when the damage was repaired.

Rachel Weigall recalls that developments resulting from Lady Rose's personal efforts were so successful that, by the time of her Mother's death on 14th February 1920, there were few organisations of religious and social work in their neighbourhood of which she was not a moving spirit.

Southwood House Convalescent Home,
St Lawrence, Ramsgate, was used as the
front of the hospital

The back of Southwood House, Lady Rose Weigall allowed the house to be used as a convalescent home during World War One.

Southwood House Convalescent Home, St. Lawrence, Ramsgate.

The front of Southwood House during World War One

CHAPTER 3 – Steinschaenau

Around about 1850, a most intriguingly named house, called Steinschaenau, was built on a large plot at the junction of Queen Bertha and Norman Roads. The site of this house, demolished over a century ago, is now occupied by Rawdon and Clarence Roads.

Steinschaenau was built for the Haedy family who were to own and occupy it until it was pulled down at the turn of the century. Its first owner, Christopher Haedy of Great Russell Street, Bloomsbury, ("the elder") died on 23 June 1859, and the house was left, shared equally between his son, also Christopher, and three daughters, Elizabeth, Anne and Louisa.

In the early 19th century Christopher Haedy was agent to the Duke of Bedford, and administered and managed his 119 acre estate in London. As well as being an astute and capable estate manager, Haedy was also a brilliant architect.

The name Christopher Haedy can be traced back to the 18th Century. A London based merchant decorator (known to be active between 1766-1781), and presumably the father of Christopher Haedy "the elder" proclaimed himself, "The German who was the first that brought the art of cutting and engraving glass from Germany". The London Directory 1808 lists Haedy & Lafont, Glass Manufacturers, 287, Strand.

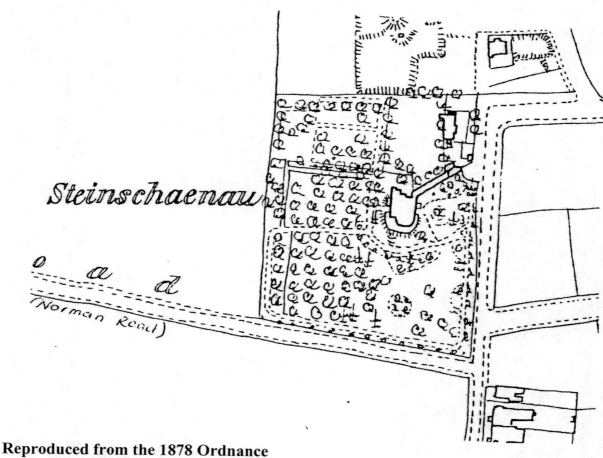

Reproduced from the 1878 Ordnance Survey map with the kind permission of the Ordnance Survey

The "Ramsgate Of Other Days" series of the East Kent Times (30 March 1938) features a charming description of the house and grounds by a Mrs J A Holness who lived in residence with the family just previous to the time the property was demolished. The house contained fourteen rooms, a very large hall and long corridors. The grounds were of sylvan beauty, and one contributor to the article remembers being taken to the Steinschaenau Estate as a child to hear the nightingale.

The house occupied a roughly central position on the land which afforded it sizeable gardens with densely placed coniferous and broad-leaved trees, an extensive path layout, and an orchard. The curtilage had a frontage to Norman Road, but the main entrance was to Queen Bertha Road. To its north, the house was adjoined by a smaller lodge. Available census records suggest no independent occupation, and although having its own grounds and access, the lodge apparently formed part of the curtilage of the main house. The servants evidently lived in the main house.

Mrs Holness described Steinschaenau as large and very lonely but lovely. The walk from the house to the gates was of considerable length. These gates were of fine proportions and surmounted by the house's striking name. They were always kept locked, but a wicket was kept open to allow communication with callers. Letters were put into a locked letter box just inside the gate, the keys to which Mrs Holness had charge. There were frequent visitors seeking alms, as the family (of the Roman Catholic faith) were noted for their charitable disposition.

The Haedy family evidently lived in considerable seclusion, and the house was surrounded by high walls. No photograph or drawing of Steinschaenau is thought to survive. In 1861 the house was too heavily shrouded by trees even to be depicted in H M Ridgeway's panoramic "Bird's Eye View Of Ramsgate". The only clues to the house's appearance are provided by old Ordnance Survey maps.

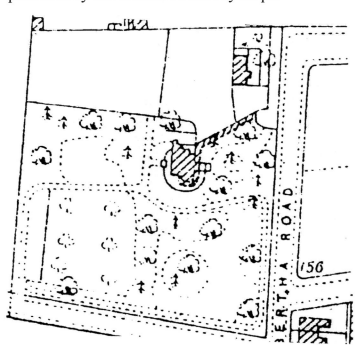

A notable feature of the house was a long, colonnade-type walk extending from Queen Bertha Road, right up to, and wrapped around, the front of the building. The plan shows that the house had what appears to have been a formidably sized front entrance porch with the wide steps up from a carriage circle. From its elevated position, the house would probably have enjoyed wide views over open farmland to the west, and a commanding sea view over "The Downs".

Steinschaenau 1898 Reproduced from the 1878 Ordnance Survey map with the kind permission of the Ordnance Survey

The architectural fashion of the period of its construction suggests that Steinschaenau might have been built in the Gothic style. Its name is almost certainly derived from Steinschonau;

17

a small town in Czechoslovakia, close to the German border and famous for Bohemian glass. It is therefore possible that the house was built in a style evocative of the architecture of that country. It is also quite probable that Christopher Haedy "the elder", being an architect, designed the house himself.

With its faintly sinister sounding name, Steinschaenau conjures up the image of a brooding pile, appropriate for the setting of a Mary Shelley novel. The number of rooms coupled with its relatively small plan footprint suggest that it was at least three storeys high. The isolated house, elevated above its grounds on a dais-type terrace, shrouded in trees, and with shady walkways, may indeed have resembled the classic haunted mansion!

Following the death of his father, Christopher Haedy (junior born around 1814), an unmarried land owner, became head of the household. In 1861 he had two servants in residence.

A terrible incident which occurred at the house was reported in the Kent Coast Times of June 1866. The article relates that one of three local children who were visiting Mr Haedy's home in Southwood, was, on being admitted by a servant, suddenly attacked by one of his bloodhounds. The servant daringly rescued the child from the dog's grip, but at this point, the other dogs present also began to attack the children. The animal that had started the attack then re seized the first child and inflicted severe injury before the servant again bravely managed to save him. By this time, Mr Haedy and several other gentlemen present arrived and were, with some difficulty, able to beat off and secure the dogs. Medical skill was summoned, and despite serious injuries, the article noted that all the children were understood to be progressing favourably. Mr Haedy was stated to have shown himself to be ready to do all in his power to mitigate their suffering and ordered that all of his dogs be destroyed.

Christopher Haedy (junior) died, a bachelor, on 18th April 1870. He died intestate, and, through the court of probate, the house passed to Anne. On her death on 21st April 1875, the house passed, equally shared, to Elizabeth and Louisa. According to census records, Elizabeth who was born around 1811 and derived her income from dividends, assumed headship. She had one servant in residence, and there is reference to an adopted child. Elizabeth died, a spinster, on 9th February 1893. On Anne's death (on 2nd April 1899), the property was held in trust for her cousin (a descendant of her father) Augustine Benedict Ricussel, who lived next to the house at number 42 Queen Bertha Road. Interestingly, the holding in trust of the property was dependent on his continuing to remain of the Catholic faith. Evidently he fulfilled this stipulation because in 1901 the house, "cottage" grounds and buildings were sold to Robert Edward Hodgeman by way of indenture between Mr Ricussel and him. The house was subsequently demolished, and the site later developed with housing (now Rawdon Road, Clarence Road and part of Queen Bertha Road). Roman remains were found on the estate at the time of redevelopment (1901).

There is still a remnant in Southwood of the house and the Haedy family. In the boundary wall between "The Ferns" and number 70 Queen Bertha Road there is a small stone inscribed, on its southern face, "CH 163 feet by 15 feet". (The reverse inscribed simply "CH"). The house had what appears to be a private but open carriageway running parallel to Queen Bertha Road. The stone was probably installed to clarify the extent of Christopher Haedy's land, and it is still there today.

Remnant Of The Steinschaenau Estate

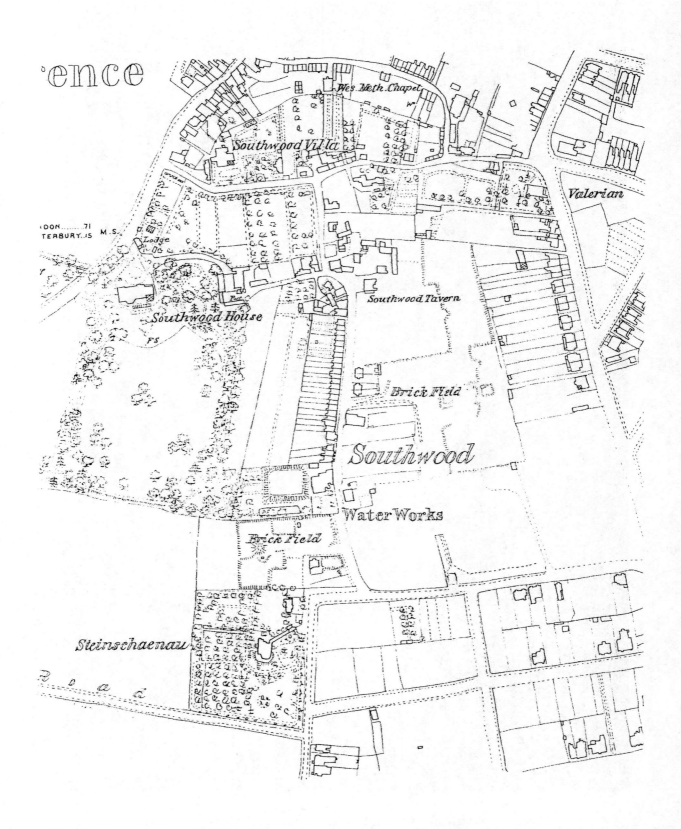

Reproduced from the 1878 Ordnance Survey map with the kind permission of the Ordnance Survey

CHAPTER 4 - Swiss Cottage

Swiss Cottage, one of Southwood's most early and charming dwellings still stands today in Price's Avenue. Following the sale of Southwood Farm, "Lot 3" was worked as a brick field before any houses were constructed on it. Swiss Cottage was the first dwelling to appear.

What is really remarkable about Swiss Cottage is that it was built somewhere else! In fact the little bungalow formerly stood at the entrance to "Elms Park" at the present site of the junction of Beresford Road with Marlborough Road, and can be seen in its original position on Ridgeway's Bird's Eye View Of Ramsgate 1861. The Cottage had to be removed to provide access to the park. Instead of being demolished, it was cut into three sections, loaded onto a wheeled, horse-drawn contraption and transported to its present site, then the disused brick field, at Southwood. The illustration below shows the Cottage being transported to Southwood. The picture was reproduced from a photograph from a Victorian "Commonplace Book" collection by a girl once resident at the Vale Tavern. The photograph is believed to have been taken at the top of Vale Road and shows the team of workers and horses together with the top-hatted owner or master of ceremonies looking out from the front porch!

Swiss Cottage moving to Southwood (source ref. 5)

The cottage was probably built around 1849, at The Elms, as the district was then called. It was occupied in 1851 by 31 year old William Bailey, his wife, Mary Anne (34) and son William Edward. As Mr. Bailey was a carpenter, it may be that he actually built Swiss cottage. Ten years later it was the home of James Minter, a lathe mender, and his wife Maria. According to census records, the dwelling was already known as Swiss Cottage in 1851, and was quite probably so named when first built. The plaque on its front wall bears the date (1866) when it was moved to its present site in Southwood.

It was sometime after Swiss Cottage's arrival at Southwood that a road was built into Lot 3. This explains why the address of the Cottage was for many years known as 82 Southwood Road, changing only very recently to 1A Price's Avenue, which it fronts onto.

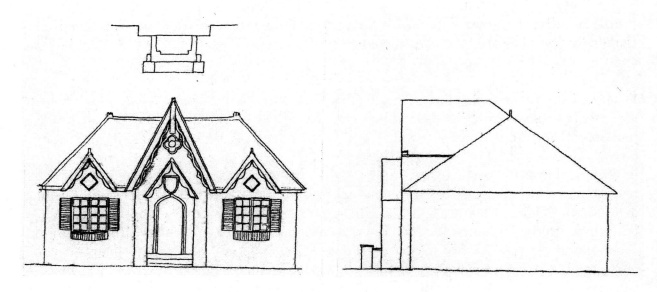

Swiss Cottage

The Ordnance Survey map dated about 1878 shows Swiss Cottage at its present site, and most of the remainder of "Lot 3" as a brick field. Bricks were probably made on site. (Several other parts of the land once comprising Southwood Farm were also worked for brick earth). The map gives a contour snapshot of the workings at the time of survey. A little mound shown on the map near the centre of the lot was probably a pile of brick earth, a small kiln or a "pug mill" for separating vegetable matter and stones from the earth. Such a mill would probably have been operated using horse power.

It is intriguing to consider why the cottage was erected at a nearly central spot on Lot 3 rather than taking advantage of direct access onto the newly formed carriageway. Perhaps this was so that its occupier could enjoy the wooded prospect around Southwood House to the north. A more likely explanation however is that some thought had already been given as to how the road frontage would be developed.

A retired butler named James Frost came to live at Swiss Cottage when he married. He and his wife Mary were the first known occupiers of the Cottage after its re-siting at Southwood. Mr Frost, who was born in Cambridgeshire, was of private means, and served as an Improvement Commissioner of the Ramsgate Local Board in the 1870's and 1880's. (see Chapter 6)

For a number of years Swiss Cottage was used as a holiday home, but has now reverted to a private dwelling. It is a picturesque little property. As a boy I used to marvel at what I then called "the witch's house", and to this day the Cottage, looks "enchanting" especially by moonlight!

CHAPTER 5 - From Hamlet To Part Of Ramsgate

Southwood

In the middle of the 19th Century Southwood comprised some sixty dwellings, many occupied by agricultural and other labourers. This included "Philpott's Row", "Workhouse Cottages" and "Southwood Cottages" which were probably in/near what later became Ashburnham and Claremont Roads. Other dwellings were addressed simply as Southwood, and that designation apparently extended from around "Southwood Cottage" (built around 1790 and still there today) in Grange Road, down to the waterworks, along what are now called Southwood and Ashburnham Roads.

While Southwood Farm had been sold by auction as building land in the middle of the Century, the 1878 map shows Southwood still as an essentially separate settlement. Many of the buildings featured are still there today, including the Southwood Tavern, Hesse Villas and Waterworks Cottages (now 75 & 77 Southwood Road), and Southwood Terrace (now 102-142 Southwood Road), with Prospect House and Poonah Villas (sometimes referred to as part of Southwood Terrace) to its south. This terrace was built around 1869 by Thomas Kittams Forwalk, probably as a speculative venture. We now go on to look at the pattern of housing development which changed Southwood from an agricultural hamlet to a residential part of Ramsgate.

Grange Road

Grange Road once formed the western "liberty" boundary of Ramsgate as separated from St Lawrence for all civil purposes after the town's association with Sandwich Cinq Port.

Grange Road. Mid 1990's (looking southwards from Admiral Fox P.H.)

The remains of an old town boundary stone can still be discerned at the foot of the flint boundary wall at the junction of Grange Road and Ashburnham Road. Its inscription eroded away many years ago, and the stone was recently truncated down to ground level. Grange Road is named after "The Grange" (Pugin's home) which stands at its seaward end. The Road generally marked the division between the old Ellington Estate and Southwood Farm. The Ellington Estate was sold for building in 1866, but its development with housing generally preceded that of Southwood, as Ramsgate grew outwards. In 1878, the inner part of Saint Lawrence (including Southwood) was incorporated into Ramsgate.

Some of the earliest buildings still standing in Grange Road lie at its northern end near the junction with Ashburnham Road. This includes the imposing Valerian Lodge, a listed building dating from about 1825, "Southwood Cottage" (circa 1790), and the Admiral Fox public house. These and other Listed Buildings near the Ashburnham Road junction form a pleasant group. Lower down Grange Road further houses and shops had been constructed by the 1880's, including the parade of six shops and the then National Provincial Bank at the Southwood Road junction. Just after the turn of the century, more shops and a dairy were built on the western side of Grange Road, between Southwood and St Mildred's Road.

Southwood Road

The present course of Southwood Road follows the line of a former track through Southwood Farm. Travelling from the Grange Road end, Southwood Road bends suddenly to the right. This bend very generally marks the point where the original Southwood hamlet meets the largely speculative housing associated with the outward spread of residential Ramsgate. Subsequent development at Southwood Road occurred at a time of significant population growth in the town, which reached over 28,000 by the turn of the century.

Southwood Road (looking west) (Source unknown)

Forty unsold plots on "Lot 2" (including Edith and Napleton Roads) were auctioned by Mr Whittingham on 3 May 1865 at the Bull & George Hotel, Ramsgate. Footways with granite kerbs were laid out in the vicinity of Queen Bertha, Edith and Napleton Roads in the late 1870's. The 1878 Map shows several houses and development plots at the lower end of Southwood Road, which later filled up with terraced housing consistent with speculative development. The name Southwood Road was probably adopted around this time, and although the entire course of the road was present by the mid 19th century, only the section running between Grange Road and Lot 3 inclusive was called Southwood Road; the remainder being known simply as Southwood.

The rest of this chapter takes us (starting from the Grange Road end) along Southwood Road and the adjoining residential roads which were developed by the turn of the Century. The houses adjoining and in Price's Avenue are visited in more detail in later chapters.

Development of the lower part of Southwood Road was "patchy". However, it was nearly all built up by 1900. It includes some terraces of pleasant and attractive character. The grandiose Plaskett Terrace (now No's 15 - 21) was designed and built by W.E. Smith; a noted architect who also owned other land around the town.

Two terraces, Plemont Villas (no's 58 - 70) and Noir Mont Villas (No's 4 - 12) named after locations in Jersey, were built at the top and bottom ends of Southwood Road around 1900 by George Goodbourne (who himself occupied no 4). Just afterwards two further terraces 33 - 51 and 48 - 56 were constructed by T.R. Tucker.

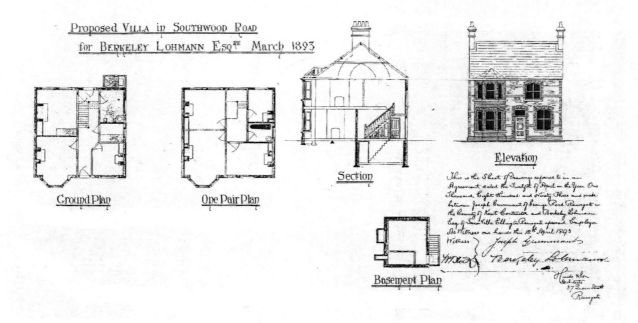

Plans of Villa in Southwood Road (source ref 6)

Southwood Road 1980's showing houses built by T. Tucker and G. Goodbourne

Bloomsbury, Lorne and Mays Roads
WE Smith had the land behind the Plaskett Terrace named "Bloomsbury Road" in 1879. This was sold in lots and largely developed up to its then extent to Napleton Road by 1900. Many of the earlier houses were designed by E. L. Elgar, a local architect. House building in Mays and Lorne Roads commenced at the same time as those in Bloomsbury Road.

Edith And Napleton Roads
Housing development in Edith and Napleton Roads began in the 1880's and Edith Road was largely complete by the turn of the century.

Seafield, Grosvenor, Herbert and King Edward Roads
Until around the late 1890's the postal address of everything north of and including Waterworks house (later 90 Southwood Road) and of Waterworks Cottages was simply "Southwood". By 1897-8 the name Southwood Road had been extended to cover its present extent from Grange Road to Ashburnham Road.

Approval of plans for the layout of Seafield and Grosvenor Roads was obtained around 1885 by Charles Buckley, a local brick-maker. Buckley built a number of the houses here. Development of these roads together with Herbert and King Edward Roads with housing was largely complete by 1900. Charles Buckley also built the terraces fronting Southwood Road between Herbert Road and Southwood Tavern, including King Harman Terrace (107-117 Southwood Road). At the junction with Grosvenor Road, one of these houses was later converted to a shop and post office. The premises remained in use as a corner shop ("Southwood Stores") until closing recently, but its familiar post box still stands on duty in the forecourt.

Southwood Stores corner shop at the junction of Southwood and Grosvenor Roads.

CHAPTER 6 - Southwood Place

By 1875, Lot 3 had been marked out with a road then known as Southwood Place (later Price's Avenue). On 27th February that year, Mr Frost (see Chapter 4) bought the land on the south side of Southwood Place, from the British Land Company. A notional building plot layout had been drawn up, and the conveyances included a schedule of stipulations for various lots including that any dwellings erected should have a minimum value of £150, that nothing except fences could be erected within 10 feet of Southwood Place and prohibiting the trade of Innkeeper, Victualer or retailer of spirits or beer to be carried on at any lot.

In 1884 Mr Frost had a substantial residence built on a plot adjoining Swiss Cottage (see "The Ferns" below). That same year, he was made an alderman under the chairmanship of the first mayor, and continued to serve the town until the time he died.

Mark Anthony Price

Either side of the junction with Price's Avenue stand several imposing Gothic-style houses. These were built by Mark Anthony Price who had bought part of Southwood Place from Mr Frost. Mr. Price, a retired glass bender, was born in Clerkenwell around 1823. He presumably came to Ramsgate for retirement as he is not listed as resident locally before 1879. On the basis that his daughter was born in Holborn it seems probable that he earned his wealth in London.

Dominique House (formerly Caroline Villa); 84 Southwood Road

Caroline Villa was built on the corner of Southwood Place (then a private road) in 1879. The house, now called Dominique House (no 84 Southwood Road) stands on the northern corner of Price's Avenue to which its original side entrance remains. A date-stone above one of the rear windows shows the year when the house was constructed.

Mark Price, an apparently popular and well to do man, built the property for himself and occupied it until 1900. He lived at the house with his wife, his widowed daughter and her two daughters and son. The family also had one young servant called Caroline Renoldson. Both Mr. Price's wife and one of his granddaughters were also called Caroline, so the house was no doubt named after one of them.

Mr Price employed a local architect: A.H. Clarke, to design the house, and the building plans were approved by the local works committee around June 1879. (Clarke later built fifteen of the houses at Grosvenor Road). There are similarities in profile between Swiss Cottage and Dominique House. It is therefore possible that Dominique House, although of grander scale was influenced by the design of the Cottage.

Dominique House is of a very attractive design, and possesses ornate sculpted barge-boards. The trefoil windows to the sides of the house's front entrance porch and the door surround to Price's Avenue entrance may be original design features, but it is possible that they were actually salvaged from another (perhaps ecclesiastical) building.

Detail To Windows - Dominique House (Price's Avenue Elevation).

Mr. Price also built the attractive and imposing pair of houses adjacent to Caroline Villa (now known as no's 86-88 Southwood Road). It is believed that he built them for occupation by his family; supposedly for his daughters. In 1884-5 one of these houses, which were then called "Twin Villas", was occupied by J. Piper: the other was unoccupied. In 1901 Mr. Price himself occupied No 1 Twin Villas; occupation of Caroline Villa then having passed to a Mr. John Barton-White.

86-88 Southwood Road (once known as Twin villas)

Frederick and Louise Villas (74-80 Southwood Road)

In 1884-85 no's 74-76 Southwood Road, (since about 1910, called Edwin Villas) were known as Frederick Villas and were occupied; No 1 by a Captain George Troup, and No2 by a Mrs. Sharp. No's 78-80 were then known as Louise Villas and were unoccupied. These four imposing semi-detached houses possess attractive barge boards and window detail. Mr. Price's grandson was called Frederick which may explain the name. It is not known where the name Louise originated from. Mr. Price is believed to have had more than one daughter and this may be why the name was used.

There are similarities in profile and mass of construction, architectural detail and perimeter walls between Frederick & Louise, Twin and Caroline Villas. But the similarities in brick banding and window detail between Twin Villas and Dominique House are more obvious, and they both have an overtly Gothic character. All of the houses possess identical metal finials and have stylised floral motifs to rendering above windows. In this latter respect, the similarities between Twin Villas and Dominique House are again more obvious.

Twin Villas, Frederick & Louise Villas were built but unoccupied by 1881, suggesting that they were erected after construction of Caroline Villa which was then occupied by the Price household.

It is evident that Mr. Price did actually build these houses rather than simply financing them. (He was listed as builder when bye law approval was obtained for Caroline Villa). The houses bear testimony to Mark Price's building skills and architectural good taste. The attractive wall and pier arrangements surrounding the houses complement their design and unify them as a group.

No's 74-80 Southwood Road - once called Frederick & Louise Villas

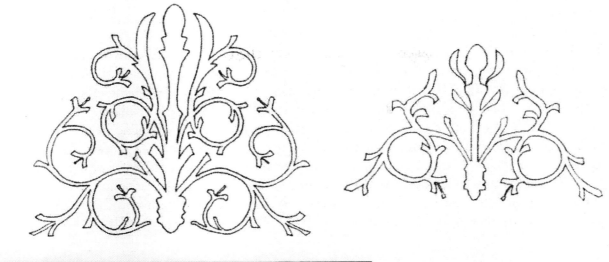

**Window detail with stylised floral decoration. Top - Dominique House.
Bottom Left 86-88 Southwood Road (Twin Villas).
Bottom Right 74-80 Southwood Road**

Mr. Price owned at least most of the northern part of Lot 3 at around this time, and it is evident that his land interests also covered the southern part of it. It is from him that the private road (Southwood Place) to Swiss Cottage was later to take its name - Price's Avenue.

Until the name Southwood Road came to apply to its present extent, the Lot 3 frontage was referred to variously as falling in Southwood Road and Southwood respectively in certain successive editions of Kelly's Directory. It is perhaps academic to question whether the first new houses erected on Lot 3 should be regarded as an accretion to Southwood, or simply as part of the outward spread of residential development from the main town. The houses had no apparent essential connection with Southwood, but were erected there before the general outward spread of Ramsgate's built-up development had reached that far along Southwood Road. At the time of their construction, the patchy building pattern was such that these first new houses on Lot 3 would probably have been considered as part of Southwood, even though it had earlier been incorporated into Ramsgate.

The Ferns

The Ferns (now 72 Southwood Road), a large, detached and attractive dwelling occupying a generous plot was built next to Swiss Cottage in 1884. The house was designed by E.L. Elgar, a local architect. It was built for (perhaps by) James Frost, who subsequently left Swiss Cottage to occupy it. At this time Southwood Place was still probably nothing much more than unmade access to the Cottage. This perhaps explains why The Ferns was erected facing the Queen Bertha / Southwood Road frontage (south) to take advantage of the existing road access there. Even so, this afforded it only some 10 feet of frontage at the point where the two roads meet at a right angle. This unusual siting arrangement gave rise to the situation whereby The Ferns and Swiss Cottage both sharing a Southwood Road address actually face opposite directions.

The Ferns - elevation to Queen Bertha Road

While the front of The Ferns faces southwards, the house also presents a pleasing elevation to Price's Avenue. This includes coloured margin lights to windows and a plaque bearing the date when the house was built. The small gateway still present in the boundary wall along Price's Avenue appears to be an original feature. So the house probably also had rear access onto it when it was simply a private road.

"The Ferns"- elevation to Price's Avenue

The houses later built on the remaining land at Southwood Place are the subject of a separate chapter (Chapter 10).

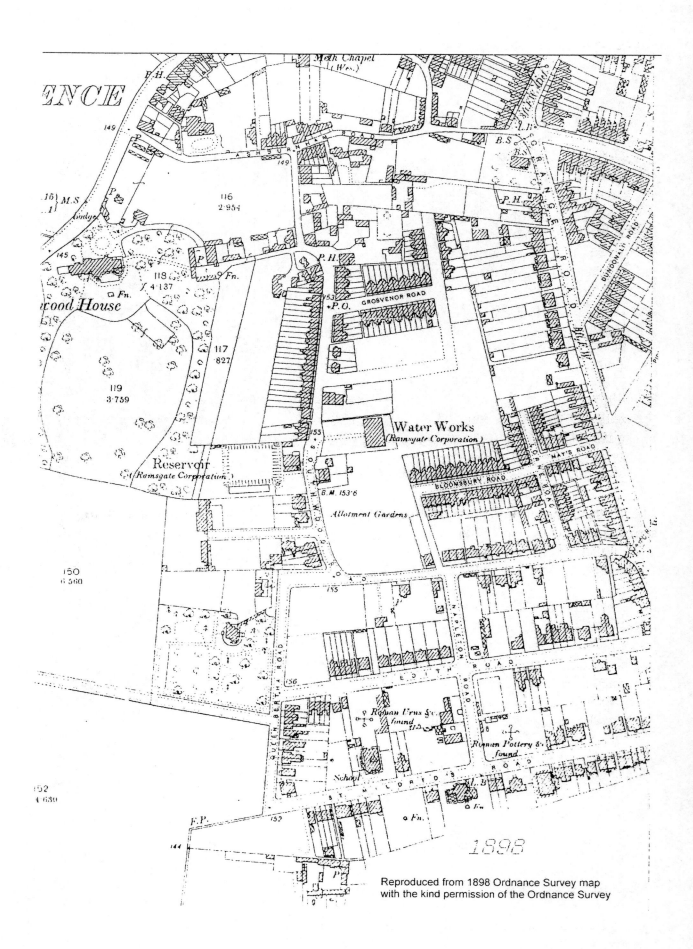

Reproduced from 1898 Ordnance Survey map with the kind permission of the Ordnance Survey

CHAPTER 7 - Football At Southwood

The origins of football in Southwood can be traced back to a point about 100 years ago when part of the land at Southwood House was given over by the Weigall family as cricket and football pitches.

There is photographic evidence of a Ramsgate Town side in 1898. Use of land at the end of Southwood Place for football had probably started by the turn of the century. The road (later Price's Avenue) was made up to provide access to it. The 1898 Ordnance Survey map shows several buildings beyond the end of the road. They stood in a small enclosure separated from the main field behind. These buildings were probably erected for agricultural purposes but were later used in connection with the football ground. Now much altered and improved, the buildings still stand at the entrance.

Ramsgate Town Football Club was reformed in 1919 and joined the Kent League. A dressing room for the club was built or converted around 1912. The Club later dropped out of the Kent league in the 1920's. Southwood Ground was then taken over by Grenville Football Club who had entered the Thanet League playing at Warre Recreation Ground.

In August 1927, the town clerk to the Borough Of Ramsgate was instructed to interview Mr. Stanley Austin of Grummants Brothers Builders, regarding the purchase of "Southwood Field" to provide playing fields. (Grummants had previously acquired the land from the Weigall family). A price of £3,000 was eventually agreed, and the field was subsequently purchased by the local authority that same year.

"Southwood Field" as purchased by the Borough of Ramsgate, evidently encompassed the entire extent of the present football ground but excluded the Norman Road frontage. Homes and Grummants builders were constructing the present houses there that same year. Price's Avenue evidently provided the only access to the ground.

A joint committee, comprising members of the recreation grounds committee and the education committee, was set up to control and manage the ground in 1928. Later that year it was resolved to lay out a full sized football pitch and school boys' league pitch together with a cricket pitch area. This included plans for use of the building to the left of the entrance as a ladies dressing room, referees room and cloakroom. Conveniences were also to be provided. The superintendent groundsman was granted 50 shillings for the purchase of a lawnmower, to be kept for use at the ground.

At this time a Mr. Philpott, a butcher at Aberdeen House, High Street Saint Lawrence, had summer grazing rights for sheep at the field. This cost him 35 shillings (70% of the price of a lawnmower!) a month. When the ground was in use his sheep were moved to the adjoining "Southwood Meadow".

In 1931, Southwood was the resident ground of Grenville Football Club. In that year the club applied to install gas to supply tea to patrons and to light the Southwood Ground dressing rooms.

After the war, due largely to the efforts of Eddie Butcher to revive senior football in Ramsgate, Southwood became the home ground of the well supported Ramsgate Athletic Football Club. With Percy Turner, later Mayor of Ramsgate, as manager, the Kent League

Championship came to Southwood in 1949/50. Improved accommodation and a covered stand were provided. Eight 40 feet high floodlighting towers were added around 1959 when the Club joined the Southern League.

The "Rams" logo.

In the 1970's the Club became a limited company under the name of Ramsgate Football Club. Today, the ground remains in the ownership of the local authority, and is the home ground of Ramsgate Football Club. One of the buildings at its entrance is used as a social club.

Southwood Football Ground just before the floodlights were replaced in 2006.

CHAPTER 8 - The Reservoir and Water Tower.

The reservoir to the north of Price's Avenue was constructed following the formation of the Ramsgate Water Works Company. A resolution to set up such a company was made at a meeting at the King's Head Hotel on 23rd October 1834. This was in response to the inconvenience and inadequacy of the existing supply, which had long been a source of complaint with visitors to Ramsgate, whose prosperity materially depended upon their opinion. It was also felt that it would be in the interests of the town's inhabitants to adopt a practical, comfortable and convenient method of supply. It was proposed that capital of £10,000 be raised from 1,000 shares.

The Reservoir

On 12th June the following year, an act was passed for better supplying with water the parish of Ramsgate and neighbourhood therefor in the County of Kent. The act noted that want of a sufficient supply was a cause of inconvenience, and increased the danger of fire. It proposed raising and conducting water from springs and sources into a proper reservoir by means of engines, cuts, tunnels, springs, conduits, feeders and other aqueducts, and thence, by pipes, to the houses and premises. Named subscribers to the company mentioned in this act included Thomas Mayhew, Joseph Templeman and John Ashley Warre.

The company was empowered to construct and maintain the necessary waterworks, buildings, reservoirs and pipe-works etc. The act also enabled it to use the piece of land (about one acre of Southwood Farm and owned by Mistress Sayer) for such purposes only, and to erect any necessary dwellings for the company's officers or agents.

The company was also required by the act to provide and maintain in Ramsgate and the adjacent parishes, a number of "fire plugs". The fire plug keys were to be left with the Surveyor of the Highways or with the (area) constables.

Hydrant standpipe which stood in South Eastern Road near the Grange Road junction. This was probably the last of the Ramsgate "fire plugs": being removed around 1986.

Following construction, the reservoir site was known as Southwood Pumping Station. Its earliest pump was almost certainly a Cornish "Bull Engine", and one of the first two steam engines to be used in Thanet. It was probably second hand. Such engines were often advertised for sale in Cornish papers when mines closed down. In this case it would have been brought to Ramsgate by sea.

In 1877 a bill was promoted in Parliament to authorise the purchase of the water undertaking from the private company. The works were handed over to the town in the following year. An order was later given to Messrs. Easton and Anderson for a new 50 HP Cornish Beam Engine with three 14 inch pumps. These were fixed in 1876.

In 1879 & 80 tunnelling was carried out in the direction of Northwood, and a constant supply of water was given to the town. By overhauling the pumping machinery, Mr. Valon (William A. Mc Intosh Valon - the town's first gas and water engineer) was able to increase efficiency by 30%. This enabled the commissioners to undertake the erection of a water tower to provide a constant supply of water to the town. The tower was designed at a height sufficient to give an efficient water pressure. This was in response to complaints from certain of the higher areas. The tower was completed in 1881 and stands on the opposite side of Southwood Road.

The tower is of red brick construction surmounted by a cast iron tank. The building is sixty feet high, and has an eighty feet by fifty feet footprint. It was built by Stevenson and Valon engineers (who also constructed the arcaded wall overlooking the harbour at Military Road). Mr. Valon the engineer was always considered to be a man who never did things by halves. The water tower, an engineering and architectural masterpiece, bears testimony to that opinion. The tank at the top which held up to 250,000 gallons, was divided into two sections so as to allow any necessary repairs without disruption of supply. The original tank has been replaced. Internally, the building is divided into five bays by arched walls, and the tank is supported on closely spaced iron girders.

By 1895, the maximum quantity of water pumped had increased to the point that new machinery and boilers were required. A new pumping station at Whitehall Road came into service in 1898. It pumped water to the tower at Southwood (which supplied about two thirds of the town) and indirectly, by overflow to the reservoir (which served the lower portion of the town).

Southwood Water Tower

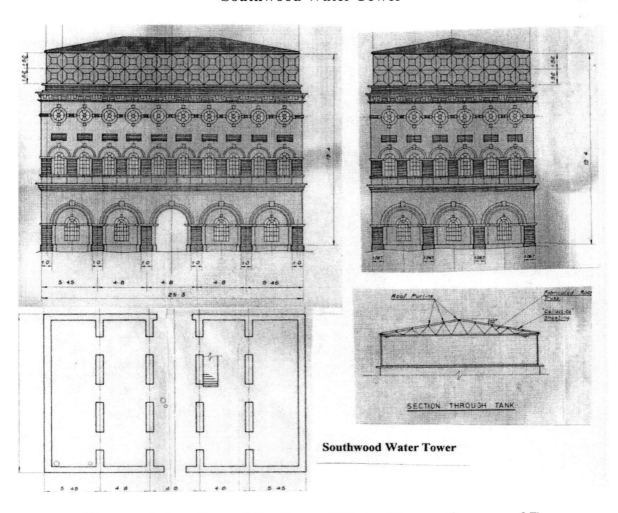

Southwood Water Tower

SECTION THROUGH TANK

Plans and elevations of Southwood Water Tower (Source ref 7)

The reservoir and engineer's house from Price's Avenue. (1978)

Plans to widen Southwood Road outside the Waterworks were submitted to the Ramsgate Improvements Commissioners in 1851. It was proposed that district rate funds be used to provide for new walls. In January the following year the works committee approved the design for iron fencing to front of the Waterworks premises, a price of 12s 3d per yard run

Fence Detail Along Southwood Road Frontage

Due to its location near the sea and resultant brackishness of the water, Southwood was, at some stage, discarded as a source of supply. Part of the reservoir site was subsequently put to use for storage and vehicle accommodation. The gardens were well maintained and were once described in a local newspaper article as a "picture in a few perches". An old cooling tank was adapted for use as an open air swimming pool for use by the elementary schools in the borough. It was equipped with diving boards, and ranged in depth from 2"6"-5"3". A number of children learnt to swim in it, and two girls once swam its 100 feet length over 30 times.

Swimming Pool next to the Southwood reservoir

The reservoir had a vaulted roof supported by some thirty columns, and was lined with tiles. The internal structure was revealed in 1998 when it was demolished to accommodate planned residential development.

Southwood Water Tower from the reservoir site. The engineer's house (no 90 Southwood Road), is to the right. The ARP warden's post (with air-attack siren on roof) was later used as a police call box. The house and call box have both been demolished and the reservoir site has since been redeveloped with housing ("Southwood Heights").

CHAPTER 9 - The Turn Of The Century

Rawdon Road

Steinschaenau had gone by the turn of the century. In 1901 R.E. Hodgeman obtained bye law approval for the layout of the two roads, (Rawdon and Clarence) off Queen Bertha Road, on the estate.

That same year approval was obtained for construction of the first six houses (no's 1 - 11) on the northern side of Rawdon Road. Kelly's Directory shows three of these as occupied in 1904/5 (Eureka (No1), Beverley (No 3), and Crispo (No 5?)); the latter being by a Captain Sidney E. Shallard. No's 1,3,5, & 7 were the first houses to be built in Rawdon Road. They have a pleasant character and possess design features typical of the average sized Victorian terraced house. Close inspection of brickwork reveals that the rest of the terrace (Numbers 9-29) was built separately.

Hodgeman's road layout probably included individual dwelling plots together with the alley network which provides rear access to the housing in Clarence and Rawdon Roads. Bye law approval for the houses in Rawdon Road was obtained by different owners for stages of 2 - 7 houses at a time. The construction phases of the houses on the southern side of the road are evident from the variation in design. The owners who obtained approval for their erection (listed below) were probably also their builders. Certain of these names are confirmed on some original drainage inspection covers remaining in the houses' front gardens.

Rawdon Road

Strangely, no's 2 - 8 were the last houses to be built. The reason for this is uncertain. The otherwise developed Rawdon Road can be seen on the 1931 Ordnance Survey map, but no clue is given as to how the site now occupied by no's 2 - 8 was then used. The absence of a number 10 Rawdon Road suggests that no's 2 -8 occupy larger plots than was envisaged before their construction.

No's 1, 3, 5, & 7 aside, the remaining houses on the northern side (no's 9 - 29), share a common design. Bye-law approval for their construction was obtained in stages, and while no direct evidence can be seen from their brickwork, it is probable that they were also built in stages. If this assumption is correct, then the nameplate "Wroxham Villas" between no's 13 and 15 implies that no's 9 and 11 -19 were built as one phase, and that the name relates to these six houses rather than the whole terrace. In 1948, no's 9 - 13 and, 19- 27 were owned by four persons, suggesting that at least half of them were occupied on a rented basis, then the predominant form of tenure.

Site	Owner	Bye Law Approval
6 houses No's 1 - 11	A. B Redman	30.05.01
2 houses No's not known	H. Parker	16.06.02
4 houses No's 13 - 19	E. Rutter	29.11.06
2 houses No's 21-23	E. Rutter	30.07.08
3 houses No's 25 -29	H. Marsh	02.09.09
7 houses No's 14 - 18 (3 built)	W.F. Clark	10.06.12
4 houses No's 20 - 26	O. Gross	26.02.14
4 houses No's 2 - 8	Grummants	23.11.34

The derivation of the names Clarence and Rawdon Roads is not known. It seems reasonable to assume that they had some association with R.E. Hodgeman. Perhaps he had connections with Rawdon in Yorkshire, and a family member called Clarence.

According to Kelly's directory 1904, R.E. Hodgeman had a posting establishment at 30 King Street, and a carrier/furniture remover company at Willson's Road. By 1937, his business had registered offices at "Smith's Yard" in King Street (R.E. Hodgeman Hauliers Ltd) and comprised haulage contractors, household removals and taxi proprietors.

By 1948 Ramsgate Corporation had decided that it would be desirable to obtain a secondary means of access to Southwood recreation ground: Price's Avenue being the only entrance/exit. The flint wall at the end of Rawdon Road had been offered but not actually conveyed to the Corporation when the recreation ground passed into the local authority's ownership. The wall was subsequently transferred to the corporation free of charge by the late Henry Weigall's trustees. A gate was installed in November 1948. In response to local concern, the Athletic Club was requested to ensure that it be used only as an exit.

Queen Bertha Road

Queen Bertha Road had been made up for some time. "Birchington Terrace" (No's 46-64) was built after bye-law approval was obtained in 1902. These houses were probably built and designed by the then landowner, G. Goodbourne: a local builder who lived in Southwood Road. These superior-style terraced houses stand on the site of the former road frontage and entrance to Steinschaenau.

Birchington Terrace, Queen Bertha Road

No's 66-70 Queen Bertha Road were built later, following bye-law approval in 1924. No's 66 and 68 were apparently built by Grummant Brothers builders and No 70 probably by E. Meddows. These houses stand on the site of the lodge to Steinschaenau.

Clarence Road
Clarence Road was named in around 1929, and its dwellings were erected in the 1930's. The four semi-detached bungalows were evidently built by Homes around 1931, and the detached house at the end of the cul-de-sac was probably by S.G. Stannard in 1934.

Terraced Houses opposite Southwood Place
The eastern side of Southwood Road, opposite the houses built by Mark Price, remained undeveloped until after the turn of the century. In 1898, Frederick, Louise, Caroline and Twin Villas looked out over allotment gardens as far as Alpha Villa (which still stands today on the corner of Southwood/Napleton Roads). By 1907 the land had been acquired by Grummant Brothers Builders, and plans approved under by-laws for the erection of seven terraced houses, which they subsequently built.

The terrace, (now No's 61-73 Southwood Road) has a two storey frontage with coal cellars beneath, and three storeys at the rear. The level of the site below Southwood Road allowed provision of a lower ground floor.

61 - 73 Southwood Road

The fronts of these houses are ornate and attractive. They are of red brick with rendered banding, and incorporate semi-circular porch entrances and parapet with mock-Flemish style gables. These features combine to present a pleasant and distinctive elevation when viewed from Price's Avenue. The glazed tiling and ornate columns, panelling and doors to entrance porches add grandeur when viewed at closer quarters.

Many of the design features of these properties bear a striking resemblance to their larger contemporaries (No's 51-59 Park Road), which overlook the town's Ellington Park.

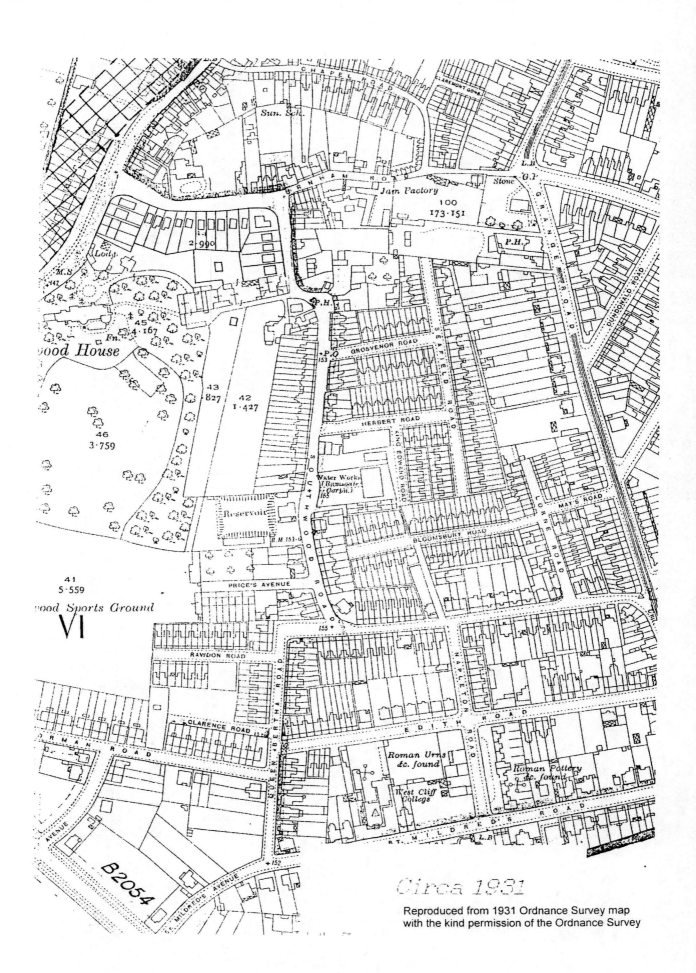

Circa 1931

Reproduced from 1931 Ordnance Survey map
with the kind permission of the Ordnance Survey

CHAPTER 10 - Price's Avenue

Southwood Farm was first sold as building land in 1847. It was nearly twenty years later, that Lot 3 was again sold at auction to a Mr Whittingham. The auction sale took place on 17 April 1866; the same year that Swiss Cottage was re-sited at Southwood. We have already noted that this land, subsequently known as Southwood Place, was worked for brick earth, and later divided into lots for development. Mr Frost bought the southern part of Southwood Place in 1875 at £30 per lot.

Following construction of houses by Messrs Price and Frost, it is unclear how the remaining land at Southwood Place was used. The 1898 Map shows buildings and enclosures just inside its western boundary suggesting farming or horticultural use. It is known that the land rear of Caroline and Twin Villas, on the opposite side of Southwood Place, was used for horticultural purposes, and in 1931 was an orchard.

Terraced Houses. Numbers 1 to 8 Price's Avenue.
Joseph Charles Grummant and Alfred Thomas Grummant subsequently acquired the remaining land on the south side of Southwood Place for house building. The conveyance, dated 12 September 1912 lists Emily Gutch Daniel, Henry Kenyon Daniel, Walter John Daniel and Mark Anthony Price, presumably as vendors. On 3rd October 1912, Grummant Brothers obtained bye-law approval for the erection of 8 houses on the site, which they promptly proceeded to construct. Southwood Place became Price's Avenue when the houses were built. It was named after Mark Price.

Mark Price had left Southwood in 1911 or 1912 to live nearby at No. 4 Ethelbert Terrace in Vale Road. He died in Ramsgate aged 91 on 19th January 1914, and was buried at Saint Laurence. Having remained in the town after leaving Southwood it is quite possible that he would have seen at least the first of the newly completed houses standing in the Avenue named after him.

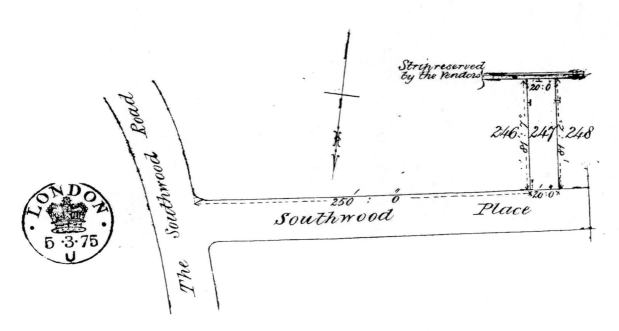

Plan attached to indenture relating to purchase of building lots at Southwood Place by James Frost, dated 27 February 1875.

The houses in Price's Avenue were built in two stages. (Construction of No's 1-4 had started by November 1912). I recall seeing a photograph of "The Ferns" taken when the houses in Price's Avenue were under construction. This clearly showed number 4 then forming the end of the terrace and confirming construction in two phases. Today the only visible clue between the two phases is a minor design variation to the terra cotta finials surmounting the gabled bays.

**Joseph Charles Grummant
(about 1929 - source ref. 8)**

1 - 8 Price's Avenue

The houses were built for rented occupation. The fact that until around 1920 No. 1 was called "Roma" (suggesting owner occupation) seems to contradict this. Nevertheless that particular property was the last in the terrace to be sold privately (in 1986) Prior to this it had been in rented occupation (by my grandfather) for some forty years. The previous occupant was believed to have been a petty officer in the navy.

Kelly's Directory of 1913-1914 shows the following occupation at the terrace.

No 1 Samuel D. Jordan (Roma)
No 3 Richard Hayes
No 4 Walter Garside

No's 5 - 8 were probably started just before or just after completion of 1 - 4. Kelly's Directory for the following year lists

No 1 Samuel D. Jordan (Roma)
No 2 Harry O. Stevenson
No 4 Walter Garside
No 5 Isaac Williams
No 6 Arthur Henry Medgett
No 7 Albert Henry Ruthven

By the time of construction of the houses at Price's Avenue, Ramsgate's population had grown to about 30,000, and was increasing significantly. The town was still a popular "watering place", with an important harbour and a commercial base.

Documentation relating to the sale of No1 Price's Avenue is understood to suggest that occupation was once tied to artisans employed by Grummant Brothers Builders. However, I have been unable to verify this. It is known that one of the other houses in the terrace was once occupied by a Miss Metcalfe; an employee of Grummants, and it is reasonable to suppose that priority of occupation could have been offered to their builders' employees. Certainly at this time Grummant Brothers (located nearby at Grange Road since 1897) undertook a wide range of work.

**Specimen Grummant Brothers
invoice dated 1919 (source ref. 9)**

Joseph and Alfred Grummant retired shortly after the houses were built, and in 1919 Grummant Brothers' business was taken over by Charles Frederick Grummant (Joseph's son) and Stanley Edward Austin.

Employees of Grummant Brothers at the store once situated at the junction of Grange Road and Crescent Road. (Probably 1920's) (source ref. 10)

The fact that the terrace was built in two stages suggests that it may have simply been a speculative venture or only partly intended for tied occupation. However it may simply have been the result of limited man-power at the outbreak of war or the builders' other work programme elsewhere. It is known that Grummants mortgaged these properties in order to finance their rolling construction programme. Mortgage conditions included their insuring the properties against fire and current war risk.

The houses are of superior construction to the average local terraced dwelling. They are also more ornate than their contemporaries, Armadale Villas; two cottages also built by Grummants at about the same time on land set back from Southwood Road adjacent to the water tower.

The Price's Avenue houses are pleasing in proportion and exhibit all the trappings of a well appointed small home. The terrace possesses a pleasant combination of detail including ornate timber railings, red brick with tile hanging and dashed rendering to upper floors. The barge-boarded gabled roofs to the bays echo the style of the older dwellings in the Avenue. No record is thought to survive as to who actually designed the terrace. Grummant Brothers are known to have prepared their own architectural designs for certain other houses built by them. However, they sometimes also employed other architects, including E.L. Elgar who designed the house (The Ferns), next to the terrace. The design

of the houses in the terrace is quite typical of that of the larger Edwardian style property. Their basic form and features were probably inspired by larger houses of similar style, examples of which can be found locally, or adapted from copy book designs.

Nevertheless their well proportioned design and intensity of detail are such as to provide the terrace with its own integrity and character and to harmonise very well with the setting provided by the older houses around the Avenue.

The ornate and distinctive style of the houses was echoed internally. Sadly much of the original detail has been lost through modernisation as the houses passed into owner occupation. However, I have been able to record much original detail from No 1, which remained largely unaltered having for so long been occupied as rented accommodation. The houses' gables and porches offer cool shade to their high ceilinged reception rooms and possess tile floored entrance lobbies. Their detail is solid and typical of an Edwardian style villa. Sunny rear gardens give warmth to the back rooms which possess a more cosy domestic quality. The upper floors of the houses have less lofty ceilings and possess something more of a "cottage" feel. Original door furniture: ebony escutcheons and knobs with brass rosettes to ground floor and iron latches to upper floors, suggest that the villa and cottage image was a deliberate design intention.

The houses, as built, included bathroom, outside WC and utility cupboard. The two larger bedrooms had built in cupboards and cast iron fire place surrounds. Fireplace mantles to ground floor rooms were timber; those to the front living rooms were grand affairs featuring fluted, Corinthian-style columns. There was a built-in dresser to the dining room. Timber work including doors, architrave and staircase furniture was unpainted but stained with a dark varnish. The original gas lamps in each house have since been replaced with electric lighting. This, together with painting of timber work means that the houses are now much lighter than when first lived in!

Within the two phases of construction there are minor variations in internal detail, including design of newel posts. No's 5-8 also possess cellars under the entrance hall area, which are accessed via the kitchen. These cellars incorporate coal delivery chutes.

Elevations And Plans Of Dwellings In The Terrace

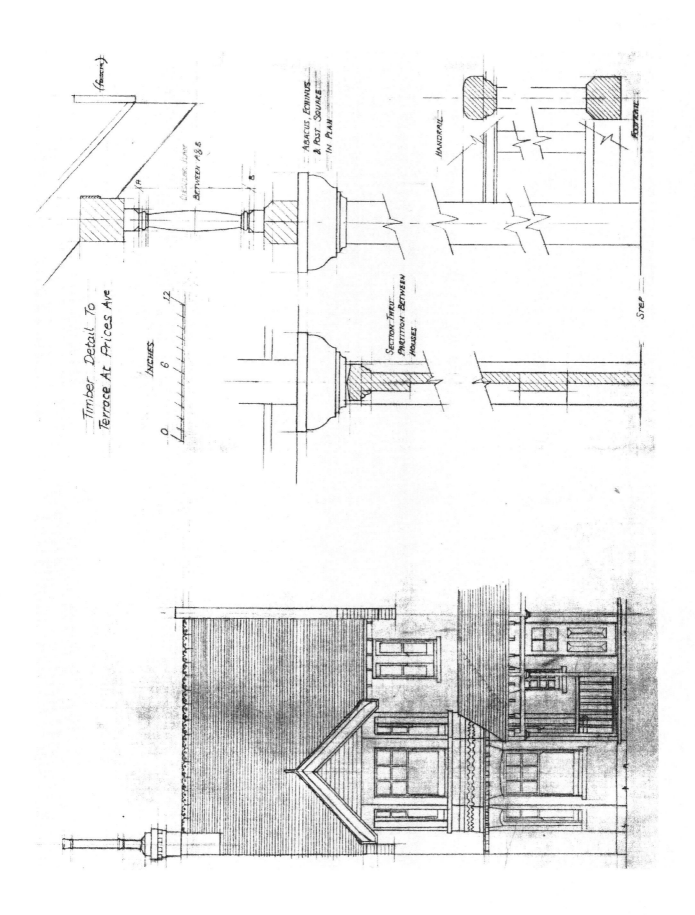

Timber Detail To
Terrace At Prices Ave

ABACUS, ECHINUS,
& POST SQUARE
IN PLAN

SECTION THRU
PARTITION BETWEEN
HOUSES

HANDRAIL

FOOTRAIL

STEP

INCHES

0   6   12

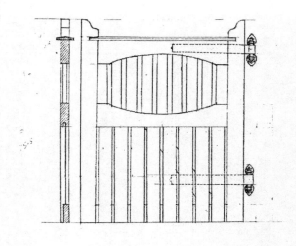

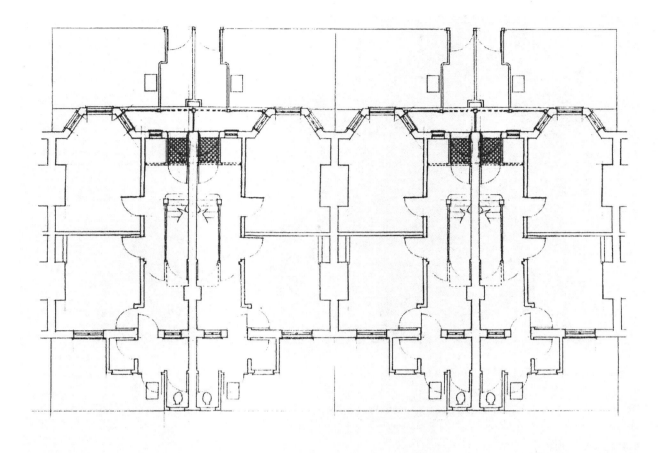

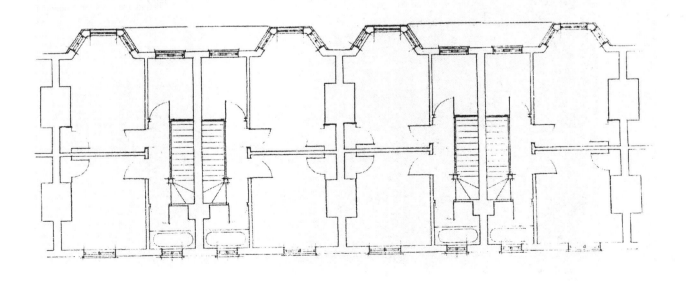

To the back of the houses, there are still portions of the original flint wall which once separated J.A. Warre's land from that of Southwood Farm. Some of the houses have been significantly modernised, others retain some of their original internal features. All of them continue to provide pleasant homes.

A Bungalow In Price's Avenue

In the early 1930's, the land on the northern side of Price's Avenue was in horticultural use, and still formed part of the curtilage of Dominique House. Some local residents remember pot plants being sold from it. (Several pear trees remain on the site, and opposite, in the garden of "The Ferns"). The land was hedged along the boundary to the Avenue. This can be seen in the photograph, which is dated around 1951. (My father is on the far right).

Price's Avenue circa 1951

The land evidently remained in such use until 1958 when Mr. E. Spain obtained planning permission for use in connection with taxi/car hire business. He subsequently bought and occupied Dominique House. Existing greenhouses were kept but garages were erected at the western end of the site to accommodate the taxis which operated from the railway station and the sea front. Lock-up garages for public use were later added.

In mid 1966 Mr. Spain obtained planning permission for construction of a large bungalow (No 9 Price's Avenue) on the land, to provide residence and office for the business. After this had been built, Dominique house passed into separate ownership.

Vehicle related business continues from the premises adjacent to the bungalow today, and although no longer run by the Spain family, many people still associate the Avenue with the family name.

The bungalow 9 Price's Avenue

Herbert John Moore and Jane Eliza Moore (nee Miles)

My grandparents, pictured above, occupied No. 1 Price's Avenue, after their previous home at 129 Margate Road, suffered bomb damage. At this time my grandfather worked for a local builder, (Ernie Taylor), and then at Dover docks to which he travelled by bus. He was called up and served in the West Ham Fire Brigade. He later worked as a labourer then stoker at RAF Manston, until retirement.

My father, Alan John Moore was born in Old Kent Road, but lived in Ramsgate from about age 3. In 1940 his school was evacuated to Stafford. He returned to Ramsgate in August 1942 and lived at 1 Price's Avenue. At the age of 15 he worked as a printing apprentice at East Kent Times. After two years army national service, he returned to complete his apprenticeship, joined the Territorial Army for a 4 year engagement, and reached the rank of sergeant on radar. In 1954 he became engaged to Sheila Easto, who was then working in Ramsgate Library. They married in 1955 at St Laurence Church, and lived at Cambridge Road in Hastings where my father had taken a job with the "Sussex Express". In 1958 they moved back to Ramsgate, and my father worked in the printing trade until retirement in 1993.

Alan John Moore

CHAPTER 11 – Post War Houses

Southwood Gardens

Southwood House was zoned for residential purposes in a local Town Planning Scheme. In 1944 the Ramsgate Town Council considered a request by the agents of the executors of the Southwood Estate to vary the scheme to increase the zoning density from eight to twelve houses per acre. However, the site had already been earmarked by the Parks and Pleasure Ground Committee for a sports ground, and there was extensive debate about the merits both of a general sports ground and the Council's "first duty to provide houses for the men who were coming back after the war". The request was granted on condition that a detailed scheme including layout, house type and elevations be subject to council approval. The houses were subsequently built around a grid-like street layout.

Fir Tree Close

Fir Tree Close was developed with housing on a layout designed by D C Heard & Co. Housing development commenced in 1948 and was essentially completed in the 1950's. Several attractive Corsican Pines, after which the cul de sac is named, remain in the garden area at the bottom end adjoining the reservoir.

Fir Tree Close

CHAPTER 12 – CONCLUSION

No's 1-8 Price's Avenue once gazed out over the wooded prospect of Southwood House, from which a rich variety of bird calls could be heard. Now the house and grounds are gone, and the rooftops of modern houses (Southwood Gardens & Southwood Heights) can be seen beyond the confines of the Avenue. The remaining Corsican pines still dominate the skyline; rare survivors or self-sown ancestors of the once wooded site.

After a booster was commissioned at Flete, both the reservoir and water tower fell into disuse. The engineer's house (90 Southwood Road) was demolished some years ago, followed by the reservoir and concrete police box, after Southern Water obtained outline planning permission for residential development. The once familiar grassed hump of the reservoir has now been replaced by "Southwood Heights", a cul de sac of houses completed in 2005.

Price's Avenue from the reservoir before it was developed

Opposite the water tower still stands; huge, indifferent and, until recently, strangely silent except for the rustle of the trees in its forecourt. The remarkable, unique architectural qualities of this Victorian landmark have been formally recognised by the Department of the Environment, and the building has been Listed as of special architectural or historic interest. The listing includes its ornate iron railings to the Southwood Road frontage. Planning permission has been granted for conversion of the tower to residential flats and at the time of writing this work is nearing completion. Adjacent to the tower, the Bendon Plastics factory building has been demolished and further houses, fronting Herbert Road, are in the course of construction.

Looking right, from the bay windows in Price's Avenue, the Victorian and Edwardian houses grouped around the end of the street present an attractive vista. Here very little has changed. They still drip with the icing and frills of their original architectural features, and retain a pleasant and distinctive character. Their detail was designed to project the image of a grand and attractive home. The Victorian and Edwardian builders were skilled in use of detail for this purpose, and it still works today. The upper part of Southwood Water Tower beyond, peeps over the tops of these houses, adding to the concentration of ornate construction, its red brick and circular windows often warmly reflecting the sunset.

The trees in Fir Tree Close and at the Water Tower are now protected under planning legislation. While there is no longer any "South Wood", the call of wood pigeons and other bird song still emanates from the canopies of the remaining trees. From the chimney pots, the cry of gulls reminds us that Southwood is not far from the cliffs and sea front.
While some change is inevitable, the houses in and around Price's Avenue retain much of their original character and provide an attractive centrepiece in a neighbourhood of pleasant character.

This history and appreciation has traced how Price's Avenue and its neighbourhood developed from agricultural farmland, and has touched on some of the more notable buildings and personalities associated with it.   It records some of the features of Southwood's distinct and pleasant environment.   Around these are wrapped many memories, emotions and perceptions of those for whom it has been a home and place to work, visit or play.   It is impossible to record human experience in the same way as architectural details, and regrettably this important aspect of Southwood as an individual place will inevitably fade as "time out of mind".

Furthermore, I cannot adequately describe my own affection for Southwood, which is redolent with memories centred around the cosy atmosphere of my grandparents' house. The tranquil tick of my "Nan's" clock, the quiet shady hall, the grandeur of the front drawing room and even the silhouette of "Grancher's" cap hanging on the kitchen door, are all part of the unique combination of ingredients that have forged personal recollections of life at Southwood. I find the flavour of these personal associations impossible to convey in writing, and the phrases will mean little to the reader. The characteristic houses in Price's Avenue are powerfully evocative "memory traps", and my affection for them, and the neighbourhood in which they stand, is mysteriously compelling.

The hall to No. 1 Price's Avenue

End Piece

I was delighted to recently make the acquaintance of Mrs S Martin (nee Barratt) who was born at no. 2 Price's Avenue (now my home) in the early 1920's. Mrs Martin's father, formerly a chauffeur, recognised Ramsgate as an up and coming seaside town and moved down to set up as joint proprietor of the "A & B" Garage in Grange Road. He resided with his partner in business in Southwood Road until the house in Price's Avenue became available at a rent of 14 shillings per week. It is pleasing to note that the house, as now, provided a happy home.

Mrs Martin's recollections brought the names of residents listed in Kelly's Directories to life and gave a delightful insight to what it was like to live in Price's Avenue shortly after the houses were built. She saw Grummant Brothers replace the original gas lighting in the terrace with electricity (at first to ground floor only). She showed us where the piano once stood. She remembered that our garden had a large apple tree and that the family kept a number of chickens. She recalled how Mr Jordan (resident at No.1) would draw pictures with his stick in the then unmade road for the children, and how, when the Jordans moved from Price's Avenue, Mrs Jordan gave all the children in the terrace (all boys except for Miss Barratt) a birthday book.

At my request Mrs. Martin has kindly provided an invaluable contribution by setting down some childhood recollections. She also provided this splendid photograph of No 2 Price's Avenue showing the terrace painted in the original Grummants livery (green, cream and white). The photograph is believed to be dated about 1930, and the gentleman in the picture is her grandfather. This and Mrs Martin's recollections provide a wonderful end-piece.

No 2 Price's Avenue (circa 1930) (with kind permission of Mrs S Martin)

CONTRIBUTION FROM MRS SHEILA MARTIN (NEE BARRATT) WHO LIVED AT
2 PRICE'S AVENUE FROM 1922 - 1939

"I was born on 27th December 1922 at No. 2 Price's Avenue to Annie and Cyril Barratt, and
named Sheila Rolling (my mother's maiden name). Our neighbours at that time were as
follows:"

No. 1 Mr. & Mrs. Jordan, and later Mr & Mrs Everett. He was a tiler at Olby's Builders'
Merchants, and they had a son Martin, and later a daughter Mary.

No. 3 Mr. & Mrs. Oliver, a retired policeman from London.

No. 4 Mr. & Mrs. Claxton of the Ship repairing Company at the harbour.

No. 5 Mr. & Mrs. Mettam, who was a bandsman in the Navy, and so was away a lot of the
time. They had a son, Leslie and a daughter, Doris.

No. 6 -

No. 7. Mr. & Mrs Fred Lyne - Motor engineer with workshops near the viaduct, Margate
Road. They had a son, Jim.

No. 8 Mr. & Mrs. Knivett - Head of Ramsgate Post Office. A son Vivienne.

"It was a happy childhood, playing the usual games (spinning tops, skipping & bowling,
hoops and hop-scotch) in the quiet Avenue. There was no traffic - just the milk cart on
which we were able to ride occasionally, and the usual tradesmen calling. Later, the Walls'
Ice Cream tri-cycle. We were all good friends, although attending different schools, and I
am still in touch with one or two in spite of us all going our different ways when war broke
out in September 1939".

Specific Acknowledgements

My wife and daughter for patience and help with typing.

My parents and grandparents for recollections and inspiring interest in Southwood.

Mr & Mrs Kendell (Price's Avenue).

Mrs Spain (Price's Avenue).

Mr George Curtis (conservation architect).

Mr Learmonth for kindly permitting survey for plan and elevations of Swiss Cottage.

Staff at Ramsgate Library (particularly the late Penny Ward).

The Centre For Kentish Studies for permission to include information from the tithe map.

Ordnance Survey.

Mr L B Austin for information relating to Grummant Brothers builders.

Mrs C.E. Busson for kind permission to reproduce 1812 illustration of Southwood from "The Book Of Ramsgate" by the late Charles Busson.

Miss P Grummant for photograph of Joseph Charles Grummant.

Mr & Mrs Furness for information regarding "Steinschaenau"

Laura Probert for information relating to Christopher Haedy

Mr R Lawson and Mr S Redman (Ramsgate Football Club information & logo).

Mr Nigel Dyer of Dyer and Sey Ltd (Eastleigh, Hampshire) for kind permission to reproduce plans of Southwood Water Tower.

The Editor - Isle Of Thanet Gazette/Thanet Times for kind permission to include photograph of Swiss Cottage from East Kent Times and to use material from East Kent Times and Kent Coast Times regarding Steinschaenau and Swiss Cottage.

Sheila Martin for childhood recollections and photograph of 2 Price's Avenue.

Terry Wheeler Editor of About Ramsgate magazine for The Ramsgate Society for the pictures on pages 14 and 15 also used for the frontispiece.

Sources - Numbers relate to the relevant references in the text

1 - Map from Ramsgate Library archive

2 - 1812 illustration of Southwood from "The Book Of Ramsgate" by the late Charles Busson.

3 Map based on various sources including 1847 auction plan (Ramsgate archive) and tythe map 1843 (with kind permission of Kent County Council - Centre for Kentish Studies)

4 Portrait of Lady Rose Weigall from "Lady Rose Weigall", by Rachel Weigall (pub 1923)

5 Photograph of Swiss Cottage reproduced with kind permission of the Editor of Isle of Thanet Gazette/Thanet Times

6 Plans of Villa in Southwood Road from Ramsgate Library archive

7 Plans of Water Tower reproduced with kind permission of Mr N Dyer of Dyer and Sey Ltd.

8 Photograph of Joseph Charles Grummant by kind permission of Miss P Grummant

9 Invoice specimen by kind permission of Mr L Austin

10 Photograph by kind permission of Mr L Austin

References

"Lady Rose Weigall", by Rachel Weigall (pub 1923)

"The Book Of Ramsgate" Charles Busson.

Kelly's Directory (various editions)

Biographical Note

Steve Moore was born in Hastings in 1956. At the age of three he moved with his parents to live in Newington Road, Ramsgate. Steve is married to Margaret, and they have a daughter, Shelley, Louise. He works as a planning officer for the local council. In his spare time Steve plays classical guitar and enjoys listening to music, admiring in particular the work of the Dutch guitarist Jan Akkerman.

PUBLISHERS NOTE

I have had considerable pleasure this week publishing Steve Moore's book and found that nearly all of the information contained in it was completely new to me. I find Ramsgate's diverse and attractive architecture of great interest, and have to admit that of our quiet residential areas often equally pleasing as that of our famous buildings.

ADVERTISEMENT

When Ramsgate library burnt down and our collection of local books was destroyed I decided that the safest way to protect scarce copies of our local history books was to produce affordable reprints of them. It's now over two years since I bought the printing equipment and started work on the project.

The books fall roughly into three categories, reprints of old books about the area that have been out of print for many years – the type of thing that one would expect to find in the local archives, directories of local people and buildings – to help you to learn more about the history of your family or house and books about this area published by us for the first time – in many cases these would never be published by a commercial publisher, nor would the authors be able to afford to publish or be able to distribute them, themselves.

Printing the books as I need them means it isn't necessary to invest a large sum in any individual publication, and that I can get on with the next one straight away. One of the local authors whose book we stock had it printed himself, 800 copies cost him £12,000, the cost of the initial print run of this book i.e. 20 copies was much more manageable. I always find it surprising that the ink costs a lot more than the card and paper.

What is really nice is that when an author comes along with a book that they have written about the local area, I don't have to produce that strange sound of air rushing through the teeth that means something very expensive is going to happen, but merely tell them that they will get a 10% royalty on the selling price of the copies I print.

Michaels Bookshop, 72 King Street, Ramsgate, Kent CT11 8NY
Open Monday-Saturday – 9.30 to 5.30   Closed all day Thursday

Postage to a UK address is free for our own publications.
We charge postage at cost to other countries and are happy to send books to anywhere in the world.

ORDERING ON THE INTERNET
Our website is MichaelsBookshop.com
ORDERING BY PHONE
(01843)589500

You can telephone us between 10am and 5pm Monday – Saturday but not Thursday with your Master card or Visa number You can also leave your Master card or Visa information on our answer phone, if you do please send a confirmatory email including shipping address.

ORDERING BY POST
Payment by cheque UK bank. Cheques payable to Michaels Bookshop

List of our publications so far

Title	Author	Price
The Ramsgate Tunnels Main Line Public AirRaid Shelter & Scenic Railway	Nick Catford	£4.99
Ramsgate in the 1900s some pictures & A Street Directory for 1900		£3.99
Pictures of Ramsgate in the 1800s		£3.99
Ramsgate During the Great War		£3.99
An Assortment of the Two Discover Ramsgate Books published in 1989/90	Don Long & George Pidduck	£3.99
A Selection of Historical Cartoons of Ramsgate	Don Long & George Pidduck	£3.99
Broadstairs in the Early 1900s Some Pictures and a Street Directory		£3.99
The Picturesque Pocket Companion to Margate Ramsgate & Broadstairs 1831	William Kidd & G W Bonner	£6.99
Ramsgate in the Mid 1900s a Street Directory for 1951 Some Pictures & a Map		£5.99
A New & Complete History of the Isle of Thanet July 1828	W. H. Ireland	£6.99
Delineations Historical and Topographical of the Isle of Thanet & Cinque Ports Vol 1	E. W. Brayley	£6.99
Delineations Historical and Topographical of the Isle of Thanet & Cinque Ports Vol 2	E. W. Brayley	£6.99
1882 Catalogue Ramsgate Gunsmith	A. T. Fitchew	£3.99
The History & Antiquities of the Isle of Tenet Vol. 1	John Lewis	£5.99
The History & Antiquities of the Isle of Tenet Vol. 2	John Lewis	£5.99
History of Birchington	J. P. Barrett	£6.99
The isle of Thanet	Edward Hasted	£6.99
The Kentish Traveller's Companion	Thomas Fisher	£6.99
The North Foreland Lookout Post in the Great War 1915 – 1917	Edwin Scoby Oak-Rhind	£3.99
Picture of Margate and its Vicinity	W. C. Oulton	£4.99
Margate in the Early 1900s		£4.99
The History & Antiquities of the Isle of Tenet Vol. 3	John Lewis	£5.99
The Ramsgate Story	John Huddlestone	£4.99
Thanet from the Air	Simon Moores	£5.99
An Isle of Thanet Directory 1849	J Williams	£5.99
Birchington & Westgate Directory 1900		£3.99
Ramsgate Street Directory 1914-15		£5.99
Petrified Haystack of Broadstairs	Bob Simmonds	£4.99
Margate and Ramsgate all About and Around Them a Gossiping Guide to Some Pleasant Places in the Isle of Thanet 1882	Chas. H Ross	£5.99
Picturesque Views of Ramsgate	Henry Moses	£3.99
Ramsgate Raids Records 1915-18	Chas. A. F. Austen	£2.99
ZZG or the Zig Zag Guide Round and About the Beautiful Kentish Coast 1897	Sir Francis Burnand with pictures by Phil May	£6.99
The New Ramsgate Guide 1897	J. Bear	£5.99
Forty Views of Victorian Ramsgate A5		£3.99
Forty Views of Victorian Ramsgate A4		£6.99
Mockett's Journal	John Mockett	£8.99
Historical Notes on St. Peter in Thanet 1904		£3.99
Breezy Broadstairs	James Simson	£2.99
Happy Family of Broadstairs	Bob Simmonds	£4.99
Ramsgate and St Laurence Street Directory 1938-39		£6.99
The War Zone In England		£3.99
Isle of Wight		£2.99
Midst Bands and Bombs	Kempe	£5.99
Greenwich Directory		£4.99
Views of Late Victorian Ramsgate		£3.99
Ramsgate's Answer	Bob Simmonds	£4.99
Ramsgate From The Ground	Bob Simmonds	£4.99
Picturesque Excursion to Southampton		£2.99
Historic Thanet	James Simson	£5.99
Photographs of old Ramsgate A5		£5.99
Photographs of old Ramsgate A4		£9.99
Views of Late Victorian Ramsgate A4		£6.99
Picturesque Views of Ramsgate A4	Henry Moses	£6.99
Broadstairs Street Directory 1971		£3.99
Ramsgate Private residents 1887		£4.99
Ramsgate Street Directory 1887		£3.99
The Antiquities of Richborough	Charles Roach Smith	£6.99
Ramsgate & Broadstairs By camera & pen 1904-5	J Bavington Jones	£6.99
Ramsgate & Broadstairs in 1890		£5.99
Broadstairs Street Directory 1950		£3.99
Ramsgate Saturday August 24th 1940	D T Richards	£3.99
Cockburn's Diary Ramsgate Life in the First World War	Ernest Cockburn	£5.99
Weather Here Wish You were Lovely A History of Holidaying in Ramsgate	Bob Simmonds	£4.99
A Corner of Kent Ash Next Sandwich	J R Planché	£9.99

Title	Author	Price
A Fateful Finger of Iron (Ramsgate Pier)	Martin Eastdown	£3.99
Adventures In Shrimpville (Pegwell)	Martin Eastdown	£4.99
Broadstairs and St Peters During the Great War	Tony Euden	£9.99
Broadstairs Harbour	Bob Simmonds	£5.99
A Collection of Old Pictures of Ramsgate		£6.99
The New Margate Ramsgate, and Broadstairs Guide 1809		£5.99
Keble's Penny Guide to Margate and the Isle of Thanet 1885		£5.99
A Walk in and About the City of Canterbury	William Gostling	£9.99
Footpaths of Thanet	Bob Simmonds	£4.99
400 Facts and Curiosities of Ramsgate	John Huddlestone	£2.99
The Romance of Richborough 1921	Lewis Shandel	£2.99
Thanet's Raid History		£2.99
Isle of Thanet Visitors Guide, 1901		£5.99
Ramsgate Directory and court guide, 1878		£6.99
Snippets of Broadstairs & St Peters	Tony Euden	£2.99
Broadstairs and St Peters During the Great War A5	Tony Euden	£5.99
3 Victorian Directories for Broadstairs and St Peters		£3.99
Memorials of the Goodwin Sands and Their Surroundings	George Byng Gattie	£8.99
An Historical report on Ramsgate Harbour 1791	John Smeaton	£8.99
The Log of a Sky Pilot	T S Treanor	£7.99
Storm Warriors of the Goodwin Sands (Ramsgate Lifeboatmen)	John Gilmore	£8.99
A Most Strange and Curious Guide to Broadstairs	Arthur Hellier	£3.99
The Cry From the Sea and the Answer From the Shore	T S Treanor	£6.99